IN THE DAYS OF THE CLOGHER VALLEY

Dedicated to my late father, who provided his own
piece of Valley history in 1937 (see page 47), and who
died on 5 January 1987 when this book was in its early
stages.

The Friar's Bush Press gratefully acknowledges the support
of Dungannon District Council, which made a financial
grant towards the book as a means of marking the centenary
year of the Clogher Valley Railway.

The Friar's Bush Press
24 College Park Avenue
Belfast 7
Published 1987
Reprinted 1991
© Copyright reserved
ISBN 0 946872 08 2

Book design—Spring Graphics, Saintfield
Typesetting—Compuset, Belfast
Printing—W. & G. Baird Ltd, Antrim

IN THE DAYS OF THE CLOGHER VALLEY

Photographs of the Clogher Valley
and its railway, 1887-1942

JACK JOHNSTON

THE FRIAR'S BUSH PRESS

INTRODUCTION

THE CLOGHER VALLEY is an area of about 150 square miles right in the centre of the nine counties of Ulster. It is fifty miles to the sea on its northern, western and eastern boundaries and its emigrants had the choice of Derry, Sligo or Newry as their point of departure. It is a region of good farmland where the northern Blackwater begins its journey towards Lough Neagh. The district, which is almost entirely in South Tyrone, takes its name from the old cathedral town of Clogher, the seat of a bishop, and in early times the residence of a petty king. At the Plantation of Ulster, Clogher became a 'Precinct' for the new settlers and was one of the four original baronies in Tyrone. The Barony of Clogher as administered by the Tyrone Grand Jury remained the local administrative unit until the introduction of the English Poor Law to Ireland in the 1830s.

Clogher Poor Law Union, which in 1898 gave way to Clogher Rural District Council, was the seat of local government in an area that comprised the five towns of Augher, Clogher, Fivemiletown, Ballygawley and Aughnacloy. This district is today's 'Clogher Valley'—a name that was seldom used before the opening of its narrow-gauge light railway a hundred years ago. The train (or tram as it was called in its first seven years), which left Aughnacloy with champagne dripping from locomotive No I, on 2nd May 1887, did much to firmly fix the identity of the area for all time.

The Clogher Valley Railway traversed a distance of 37 miles altogether, and ran between Maguiresbridge in County Fermanagh and Tynan in County Armagh. Although the track distance in the Valley is about 20 miles, the whole course of the line is sometimes misleadingly termed the 'Clogher Valley'. The C.V.R. linked up with the Great Northern system at both ends and in doing so gave the people of the Valley access to wider horizons as well as bringing in a whole range of new goods for their consumption. It was a leap towards modernisation that has been as significant as the extension of the MI to Dungannon eighty years later. The railway age here lasted for 54 years until competition from road traffic forced its closure on 1st January 1942. It is these years that set the framework for this book—a glimpse at the life and people of the area between 1880 and the years of the Second World War. It is a look at the railway, at its towns and villages, at farmlife, at its industry (limited though it was), at its people and their pastimes in the 'days of the Clogher Valley'.

The structure of society in the Valley and the pattern of life generally is largely a result of the reorganisation of land at the time of the Plantation. The Clogher Valley or Clogher Precinct was O'Neill territory before then and as early as 1261 one of the family was in possession of the castle at Augher. They ruled the area until 1603 by which time they were in control of the whole Blackwater valley from Fivemiletown to Benburb. Elizabeth I confirmed them in possession in 1578 when she made Turlogh Lynagh O'Neill 'Baron of Clogher', following the English policy then in favour of granting English titles to Irish chiefs. It was from the O'Neills and their undertenants, the McGirrs, Quinns, McRorys, Keenans and Hagans that the land was confiscated by the Plantation commissioners in 1610. These escheated lands were, with one exception (at Carnteel) granted to English Undertakers and Servitors. Few of the English were able to fulfil the terms of their contract with the result that by 1641 the settlers both at landlord and tenant level were mainly lowland Scots. By the end of that century the area was largely controlled by five Scottish families, the Stewarts or Mountjoys at Aughentaine, the Erskine heiresses (one of whom married the first Moutray of Favour Royal, and the other, the first Richardson of Augher Castle), the Hamiltons of Ballygawley, the Moores of Aughnacloy and the Cairneses of Cecil and Killyfaddy.

Some early leases and the Hearth Rolls (1666) show that while the Irish population lost most of their lands they still remained in the area. They moved onto the poorer soil and marginal farmland often above the 500 foot contour. As time passed many were able to return to the better farms along the floor of the Valley mainly because the new landlords were unable to find enough English or Scottish tenants to farm the land. Nevertheless it was basically true that the majority of the good land was, and remained in Protestant hands while the Catholic population existed in the higher areas and on the poorer tracts. In modern farm practice it is a dichotomy between the 'infield' and what has been aptly termed the 'Less Favoured Area'.

Most of the population in the Valley derived their livelihood from farming, which in the span of this book was a type of mixed farming with a high percentage of the land under crops. The second half of the nineteenth century was characterised by a marked decline in tillage, in this case from about a fifth of the land area in 1860 to about a twelfth or about 8,000 acres by 1900. Oats, potatoes and flax were the main crops and there was some wheat and barley as well as a steady acreage of turnips. Hay was saved for winter feeding and by the end of the 1880s some of the gentry had embarked on silage making in stacks or pits. Cattle raising, with an increasing preference for the Beef Shorthorn, was an essential part of the larger farmer's economy. Pigs were popular on the smaller holdings and sheep were to be found on the landlord's demesnes or on the larger acreages of the

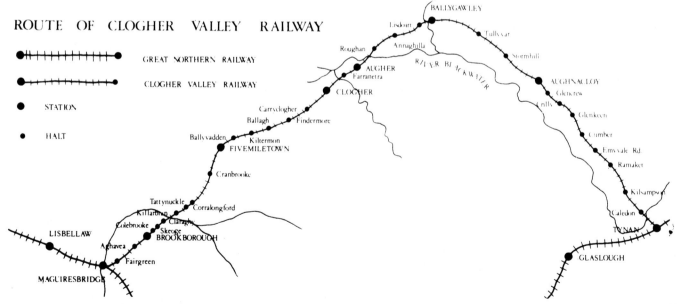

ROUTE OF CLOGHER VALLEY RAILWAY

GREAT NORTHERN RAILWAY

CLOGHER VALLEY RAILWAY

● STATION

• HALT

V

gentlemen farmers. Ballygawley cattle fair was in its day one of the best in Ireland.

Farming methods were remarkably up-to-date considering the distance the area was inland. Many of the larger farmers were quick to import new machinery, and Ayrshire-made ploughs and reapers had appeared by 1900. The smaller holdings still relied on spade labour and on ploughs made by local blacksmiths. A lot of labour was hired by the half year and in 1900 it was not unusual for a farm of 30 acres to have both a man and a girl employed. When the 1901 Census was taken one large farm at Lungs returned six hired servants living-in. Nearly every farmer possessed a scots cart—either to suit horse or donkey, and on the larger farms this was complemented quite often by a dray cart or rick shifter. On Sundays these men drove to church in gigs or roundabout traps.

The Valley had little industry beyond that which was connected with agriculture. Twenty corn mills and thirteen mills for scutching flax provided employment for no more that about 200, while the thirty forges which supplied a range of gates, farm machinery and cart axles employed about a further hundred. Two of these forges were spade foundries and at one time the locals had a choice between purchasing a 'Gorman' or a 'McNelis' as well as the ubiquitous 'MacMahon'. Tom Martin of Aughnacloy was another specialist in this field, and, as well as producing the much sought after 'Martin' plough, he built churning machines and threshing mills. There was a small Art-metal industry at Fivemiletown by 1900, where a group of artisans under the direction of Mrs H de F. Montgomery of Blessingbourne made items in copper and brass. There was a brewery and a distillery in Ballygawley in the nineteenth century though by 1880 their day was almost over. Lisdoart Spinning Mill, erected in 1864, was the one big industrial enterprise that was

Fair Day at Ballygawley, *c.*1924

still flourishing when the railway opened. It employed over 200 in producing flax yarn and was on the same site as a ropewalk.

The community was serviced by five towns, the three new post-Plantation settlements of Aughnacloy (built by the Moores), Ballygawley (built by the Stewarts) and Fivemiletown (developed by the Montgomerys) as well as the two older former boroughs of Augher and Clogher. These towns and villages were places of greater importance than their size suggested. All were market towns and the term 'village' was not applied to any of them until quite recently. As well as being centres for fairs and markets they provided a basic retail service. Linen was important in the area before the Famine and Aughnacloy and Ballygawley were thriving centres for cloth and yarn. More than half of the farm labourers were weavers during the winter months and even after the decline of the industry here the number of spinners remained high as their womenfolk still spun for other centres. The towns provided other facilities as well. Banking and insurance was centred there as were the medical dispensaries. The hire of post cars, which was so important to the commercial traveller, especially in the pre-rail days, could be had from each town, or from its hotel. The railway made each town an important depot for the shipment of goods as well as livestock. There were sidings to the two creameries and to the pork weighbridge on Fivemiletown fairgreen.

The towns were important focal points of social life for it was here that most social contacts were made. The majority of the population walked to town on Saturdays to buy their provisions, with some staying long enough to spend their wages in one of the forty or so spirit-grocers. Before the building of church halls many of the local organisations used the licensed house as a meeting place. By the turn of the century this had changed and the Freemasons, the Orangemen and the Hibernians generally had a hall in each village. The Orange Order was so strong that its halls were dotted through the countryside as well, and tiny—often corrugated-iron halls at Timpany, Lislane, Glenageeragh, Loughans and Killyfaddy illustrated the strength of the Order in the Protestant community. Most of the towns had two or three churches representing the different denominations that existed. Indeed there was such an interest in religion that when splits occurred additional church buildings followed. Aughnacloy and Fivemiletown once had two Methodist churches each.

There was little interest in leisure among the farming community until fairly recently. Sport was considered a waste of time by most until about 50 years ago. Despite this there were association football teams in most towns, Gaelic football in three of them, golf (though intermittently) also in three, cricket in two and hockey in two. Athletic sports organized at parochial level were also popular. There was considerable interest in handball and the advent of the bicycle provided a new outlet for open-air enthusiasts. Horse jumping and horse racing was popular with the gentry and the gentlemen farmers. In its early days the railway ran excursion trains to race meetings at Tynan and Aughnacloy. It was the annual ploughing matches which probably created greatest interest in the agricultural community. There was a Clogher Union Farming Society in the 1860s, a South Tyrone Farming Society in the 1890s and a third—the Clogher Valley Agricultural Society—in this century. It has been promoting agricultural shows and gymkhanas each year since 1904. The Clogher Valley Show quickly became the principal 'day out' for all sections of the community.

THE PHOTOGRAPHERS

ONLY FOUR OF the photographs in this selection were taken by professionals. One is from the collection of W. A. Green, two are by Alexander Hogg and a fourth was taken by R. J. Welch. Three others could well be the work of the celebrated William Lawrence. The Valley's photographers ranged from Rose Shaw—a governess who lived at Fardross and who used a large and sophisticated camera—to local enthusiasts working with small box cameras in the inter-war years. There were others who were semi-professionals in that they earned part of their living from studio portraiture. These included Mary Martin of Ballygawley, whose work dates from about 1910, Sidney Williams of Fivemiletown and the Tierney brothers also of Fivemiletown who were watchmakers as well. Probably the earliest photographer at work in the Valley was another Fivemiletown man, Noble Gillespie, who is listed as a photographer in the Tyrone Directory of 1872. Gillespie was a grocer and baker and in later years seems to have given up studio portraiture. His son, W. J. Gillespie, was well known to many when he was the owner of the Valley Hotel in the 1920s and 1930s.

Pat Tierney was probably the most versatile. He used to take his camera on the train and travel to the homes of farmers to photograph their families. He usually spent a whole afternoon with one household, moving on to a neighbour's place for an evening session before returning to Fivemiletown on the last tram of the day. Sidney Williams also moved around with his camera and was the chief recorder of the various Fivemiletown football sides and their trophies. He died in 1935. Others who took some photographs in these

Sidney Williams in action at Fivemiletown, 1922.

years were Miss Gladys Moutray of Summerhill (later Mrs Johnston of Omagh), D. N. McClure, a Scot who in 1922 was appointed Mechanical Engineer (and subsequently General Manager) of the Clogher Valley Railway Company, Dr George Gillespie, who was appointed Medical Officer in Ballygawley in 1932, and Alec. Bennoch of Fivemiletown, who ran one of the first motor garages in the district.

It is the work of two of the ladies which is perhaps the most intriguing. Rose Shaw was appointed a governess to the family of Moutray Gledstanes of Fardross House about 1888. After her young charges had grown up her services were no longer required and she returned to England. She retained close ties with the Gledstanes and came back to Fardross most years for a month's holidays. It was in these years at the beginning of this century that her photographs were taken. Her work was from a small area—the part of Clogher mountain above Fardross to which she could easily walk on foot. She used a heavy plate glass camera and tripod and generally paid a young boy sixpence a day to carry it for her. In 1930 she published her *Carleton's Country* (Talbot Press, Dublin) which described this area and its associations with the famous local-born nineteenth century novelist William Carleton. It included sixteen of her photographs. Her subjects were the mountain farmers and their families by their firesides, working at turf or in their fields. It is now generally recognised that much of her work was posed for, as one old man put it to me recently, "she bought the childer with sweets and the men with chews of pigtail tobacco." Rose Shaw nevertheless captured a way of life that even in this area was changing quickly and which without her would never have been recorded. She lived to a great age and died in Bath about 1949.

Mary Martin was the wife of Hugh Martin the Permanent Way Inspector with the Railway Company. They came to Ballygawley shortly after the line opened and set up a small hotel and drapery shop in Ballygawley. This seems

Hugh and Mary Martin, Ballygawley, *c.*1925.

to have been more Mrs Martin's preserve than her husband's and from about 1910 she was operating as a photographer as well. She published a series of postcard views of local places and did a useful business in portraiture. Hugh Martin relinquished his post with the Railway Company in 1928 and shortly afterwards the couple moved to Bangor where they spent their retirement.

THE RAILWAY

THE CLOGHER VALLEY RAILWAY began its life as a tramway, and was built under the Tramways and Public Companies Act of 1883. The line was laid down in 1885 and 1886 and was opened to traffic on 2 May 1887. Although the Company failed to make a profit in the first seven years, its promoters were undaunted and in July 1894 changed the name to a railway. Initially there were six steam engines—small tramway engines fitted with a huge headlamp and a cow-catcher. They were supplied by Sharp Stewart of Manchester and, in railway parlance, were of the 0-4-2 type. The line ran alongside the public road for much of the way and to ensure better safety the engines ran backwards as there was a better view from the cab. They were also fitted with hinged flaps over the wheels to protect animals from getting caught up with trains in motion. The six little engines were extremely durable and three of them were still in service when the line closed.

The engines were named after three local rivers—the Blackwater, Fury and Colebrooke and after three places of local importance, Caledon estate, the ancient parish of Errigal Keeroge and Lough Erne where the western terminus, Maguiresbridge, stood. A seventh engine, named Blessingbourne, was added in 1907 while in 1934 one of the engines from the Castlederg and Victoria Bridge line (which closed that year) was purchased to replace the 'Caledon'. It was rebuilt by the Company in the Aughnacloy works and named the new No 4. However, by now steam was on the way out and in 1932 the directors obtained two diesel units, a 28 seat railcar for passengers and one with a lorry body for freight. The limiting of steam operations proved to be something of an economy and enabled the line to survive until the Second World War.

The rolling stock consisted of 13 passenger coaches, 6 parcel and brake vans and just over a hundred assorted goods wagons—ranging from horse boxes to butter wagons, but of which the majority were designed for the movement of cattle to and from the fairs. The bulk of the freight, apart from cattle, was timber, coal, meal and farm produce. There were trains carrying the mail and supplies to the shops—including barrels of Guinness—as well as those like the milk train which provided an essential daily service for the farming community. The passenger coaches ranged from the luxurious first class carriages with inlaid wood panels and leather upholstery to third class with its plain perforated wooden seating. On busy days like the Twelfth of July or the Clogher Valley Show some of the wagons were fitted up with benches to accommodate the extra passengers. These 'specials' often needed two engines, and occasionally a third, pushing to get the train over Tullyvar hill. This ordeal may have given rise to the story where the guard ordered the First Class to stay where they were but the Third Class passengers to get out and push!.

Engine No 6 *Erne* at Aughnacloy. The cow-catcher and hinged
panels over the wheels were designed to protect wandering
livestock from getting caught up in the engines. A first class
carriage with clerestory style roof and open verandah is clearly
visible.

Tynan *c.* 1910. The *Caledon* arrives with a Clogher Valley train while a Great Northern train stands in readiness at the other platform. The Clogher Valley used the GNR facilities at both Tynan and Maguiresbridge and did not have its own stations. It had, however, goods sheds at both and a locomotive shed here at Tynan.

After a mile the CVR reached Caledon, where the track ran
along the centre of the village street. Here the *Erne* makes its
way up Caledon's street which was decked out for a royal visit
in 1934.

Emyvale Road halt 1923. The A Specials check out the train *en route* for Aughnacloy.

Aughnacloy, which was 9½ miles from Tynan, was the Company's headquarters. The goods shed and engine workshops provided considerable employment locally. The station, which housed the boardroom on the first floor, is hidden in the trees on the extreme left.

Twelfth of July morning at Aughnacloy.

Aughnacloy workshop staff *c.* 1936. Back row, left to right, Joe McAree, Robert Barrett, Joseph Robinson, Walter Wright, Hugh Murphy and John McKeown. Front, Pat McFadden, James Friel, Willie Rea, R. J. Gillespie, John Girvan, J. Brown and R. Rea (Photographer, Denis Robb).

From Aughnacloy the train headed for Ballygawley over
Tullyvar hill. Here John McKeown flags a train from
Fivemiletown across the road at Dempsey's Crossing.

Shunting at Ballygawley. The hut on the right is part of the
Permanent Way workshop.

In Augher the railway ran across the Main Street. This photograph taken in 1900 shows the train leaving the station which was adjacent to the old market house (the white building), the upper floor of which served as a Petty Sessions court.

Augher Station *c.* 1903. The group includes the stationmaster,
W. J. Robinson (under the lamp), his wife, mother and infant
son, Victor. The market house is in the background. At Augher
there was a siding to the Creamery.

Clogher Station with the *Errigal* arriving from Tynan. The goods shed is on the left. At Clogher the line diverted from the road for about two miles, in order to avoid the hill on which Clogher is built.

Another view of Clogher Station. The water tower is gone now.

On the way down into Fivemiletown the line passed close to Blessingbourne estate which was the home of the Rt Hon. Hugh de F. Montgomery, one of the principal promoters of the Company. The new engine purchased in 1907 was named after his estate. Here the engine is photographed at Aughnacloy in 1912 with the workshop staff. They are: on footplate—Joe Irwin with the driver W. J. Thompson; standing along the side are (left to right) John Cuddy, Mick McFadden, Robby Boyle, Jas Friel, Archy Given, Dick Bennett, Joe Patton, Ed O'Donnell and John Conn (Stationmaster). At the back of the engine are Ted Kemp, Willie Armstrong, Ferris Martin, Charlie Meenan and Thomas Owens. Seated in front are Pat McFadden, William Rea, John Owens, young Tottenham Armstrong and Mick Cullinan.

Often the approach to Fivemiletown was blocked by Maggie Coulter's goat. The fireman generally had to pelt it with live coals to clear the line, with the result that Maggie Coulter was hardly ever short of a heart for her fire!

Passing the Fair Green (on right) and Bell's Shop, on the way
to Fivemiletown Station.

Porters and staff at Fivemiletown Station *c.* 1936. The
Methodist Church can be seen in the background.

After Fivemiletown the line passed close to Colebrooke estate where there was a station. Engine No 5 pictured here took its name from the estate and from the Colebrooke river which it crossed here. After Colebrooke the line completed its route to Maguiresbridge, stopping at 3 further halts as well as at Brookeborough station.

The *Erne* with drivers and workshop staff *c.* 1920. Standing (left to right) Gustav Akerlind (Locomotive Superintendent) Walter Abraham, James Wilson, Dick Irwin, Bernard McClean, Ted Kemp, Tom Carbury, Pat McFadden, Geo. Wright, Jas Friel, John McDowell, Moore Burton and John Emerson. Kneeling (left to right) Dick Bennett, Joe McAdam, unknown and a young David Stinson. Wm Irwin is the driver in the cab and John Girvan the fireman to the front of the engine. George Leaney, another driver, is by the lamp.

The *Castlederg* engine, purchased by the Company in 1934 and
rebuilt as the new No 4 at Aughnacloy.

The Diesel Railcar at Aughnacloy before its inaugural run in
December 1932. Sir Basil Brooke, who was then Chairman of
the Committee of Management, is seen talking to D. N.
McClure, the General Manager. The railcar was later sold to
the Co. Donegal Railway and today is in the Belfast Transport
Museum at Witham Street.

The line was closed on 1st January 1942, and at the auction in the following April the three Sharp Stewart engines which remained fetched between £115 and £125 each.

Clogher Valley Railway

Obituary, 31st December, 1941.

The end of it all. Track lifting gang at Clogher station yard,
May 1942.
(Photograph Miss Ruby McKeown)

Abridged version of ballad
composed by E. O. Byrne, then
cashier in the Ulster Bank, Clogher.

They tuk our ould railway away, so they did,
And Sowl' the whole thing for a few thousand' quid.
They say now the ratepayers here are well rid.
Ahmdambut, boys it's tarrah.

For fifty long years past she puffed to and fro,
And whiles she wud get there at ither times no,
She's worth far more dead nor alive, so must go.
Ahmdambut, boys it's tarrah.

She run down back gardens an' up the Main Street,
And frightened the horses she happened to meet,
And now she's been tuk off tae build up our Fleet.
Ahmdambut, boys it's tarrah.

They say they are sellin' the ould line for scrap,
The rails will make bombs for till plaster the map,
Here's hopin' ould Hitler's below when they drap.
Ahmdambut, boys it's tarrah.

It's said that the R.A.F. soon will begin
To use up our railway, this war for tae win,
They'll drap Clogher station all over Berlin.
Ahmdambut, boys it's tarrah.

When the Roosians an' us march down Wilhelmstasse,
Ould Hitler will surely say, ''Boys, I'm an ass,
I might have knowed Clogher could still 'hould the pass'.''
Ahmdambut, boys it's tarrah.

Clogher.   ''OMEGA''
May, 1942.

Towns And Villages

THE TOWNS of the Clogher Valley—it would be almost impertinent to use the word village—were all bustling places in the days of the Railway. The CVR Company quickly recognised this and ran specials for fair and market days. When the line opened in 1887 Aughnacloy was easily the largest and most important town on its route. With a population of 1,333 in 1881 Aughnacloy was nearly as big as the other four towns put together. Each of the Valley's five towns had its 'place in the sun' over the years. The two older former boroughs of Augher and Clogher had their heyday in the seventeenth and eighteenth centuries while Ballygawley made its mark in the early years of the nineteenth. Fivemiletown remained a small place until about 1820 when it began to expand rapidly. Today it has finally overtaken Aughnacloy in size and has now become the busiest of the Valley's towns.

Aughnacloy was built in the first half of the eighteenth century by Acheson Moore an enlightened landlord who had just returned from spending eight years in Europe doing the 'grand tour'. He laid out a splendid wide street and aimed to call his town 'Mooretown'. He succeeded in it for only a brief spell and was not long laid to rest before the locals reverted to using 'Aughnacloy'. The main thoroughfare, however, is called Moore Street today and three of the side streets are named after his three wives (not his daughters as many seem to think). Moore built the parish church in 1736 and established a linen market in 1762 just eight years before his own death.

In the next hundred years the town grew steadily and by 1821 it was the second town of Tyrone—after Dungannon, the county town. A bank was opened by James Falls as early as 1804, and in 1818 an important business foundation was laid when the young James Fiddes became the junior partner of James Simpson, then a prominent woollen draper. Fiddes was the "Acheson Moore" of his day, and at the height of his career about 1850 was operating a large enterprise, a wholesale grocers, the drapery with the Simpsons, a wine and spirit business, a corn mill, a seed market and the Aughnacloy Mineral Water Company as well as manufactory of snuff! Largely through his efforts Aughnacloy was created a town under the 1854 Town Improvement Act. Nine commissioners were appointed to regulate fairs and markets and with the right to strike a local rate. Through it they provided gas street lighting and had the town paved with Caithness flags. Aughnacloy became the headquarters of the Railway in 1887 and as well as having the largest station, had a locomotive shed, workshops and a marshalling yard not far behind those of Dundalk.

Augher's early history was tied up with its strategic importance as an O'Neill castle. Donald More occupied Augher in 1261, and his descendants were still there in 1602 when it fell to the English. At the Plantation the town was created a borough and returned two M.P.'s to the Irish parliament over the next 200 years. In the early 1700s Augher was the Valley's leading settlement with its tuck, corn and flax mills as well as its tanyard and small distillery. As its resident landlords gradually became impoverished so did the town with the result that the Ordnance Survey Commissioners in the 1830s saw it as "mean built and miserable". However new landlords later in the century gave it new life. Two churches were erected in the 1860s and the corn and flax mills were rebuilt. John Carmichael-Ferrall also built a saw mill and was one of the chief promoters of the creamery which opened in 1898.

Clogher was the oldest of the Valley's settlements. It became the seat of a bishop in the fifth century and was the site of a mediaeval monastery. By 1395 it contained a cathedral, monastery, two chapels, a bishop's palace and 32 other houses. It was burnt the following year, and on a number of other occasions during the O'Neill wars was partially destroyed. The bishop, who was also the local landlord, rebuilt his town after each raid. An account written in 1628 described the town as "an old and auntient city decored with twoo churches and a great number of inhabitants [but which in] the late warres was utterlie ruyned". Bishop Spottiswood rebuilt the town at the time of the Plantation when like Augher it became a borough with its own corporation. Despite this it remained a small place until the appointment of Bishop Garnett in 1758. He was the first resident prelate for many years and did much to improve the town. The market house and diocesan schoolhouse were built by him, and he made strenuous, though unsuccessful, efforts to make the latter a grammar school. In the early nineteenth century the place was improved and developed by the brothers John and Joseph Trimble who had acquired considerable freehold property. Joseph Trimble and his son, George (later to take the name Brackenridge) eventually came to own almost half the premises on the Main Street. The opening of the Workhouse in 1843 made Clogher the administrative capital of the district. The family firms of Steens and Johnston Brothers played an important role in introducing the latest implements for the farming community, the former in the late nineteenth and the latter in the early twentieth century.

Fivemiletown was a small village until the arrival of Col Hugh Montgomery to live at Blessingbourne in 1810. Between 1821 and 1837 he almost doubled its size, and built most of its public buildings as well—the Petty Sessions House, a police barracks, a school and the Shambles. Little further progress was made from then until his grandson, Hugh de Fellenberg Montgomery, took up residence in 1870. He provided a new butter market, a dispensary and an attractive new school designed by an eminent English architect. About the same time the creamery was set up and the Northern Bank opened a branch. Montgomery was one of the principal promoters of the Railway and narrowly failed—along with David Graham, to make Fivemiletown the headquarters of the Company. At Fivemiletown there was an extensive goods yard, an engine shed, stock pens and a siding onto the fair green for the use of the new pork market. Like her husband, Mrs Montgomery took a keen interest in the town's welfare. She founded 'Fivemiletown Industries' (See page 60, and photograph on page 62) where a group of men worked in copper and brass making dishes, racks, fenders and other ornamental items.

Ballygawley like Fivemiletown, was largely the product of an interested resident landlord. Sir John Stewart, who completed his purchase of the Ballygawley estate in 1811, was the first proprietor for well over a hundred years who was not an absentee. Within twenty years he had doubled the town's size and almost doubled its population as well. Stewart re-established its once highly prosperous and well attended linen market, instituted monthly fairs and built a market house. There was a brewery and distillery in these years—run by the Armstrongs—and a small glove making industry. The fairs prospered and by the end of the nineteenth century Ballygawley had become one of the premier cattle fairs in Ireland. The Railway was a great benefit to the town and its cattle fairs in particular, as the animals were sent off by rail for shipment on the cross channel boats from Belfast. John S. Gervan who ran the Stewart Arms Hotel was the main advocate of the Railway locally. He realized its potential and in 1888 had the hotel completely modernised, providing acetylene gas lighting, an electric bell service, telephone and heating by hot water pipes. Gervan's car met all trains and the passengers travelling First Class were assured of the comforts they were used to when they reached his hostelry.

Aughnacloy from the Monaghan Road *c.* 1927. St James's
Church built by Acheson Moore in 1736 dominates this view.

The Egg Market in Aughnacloy *c.* 1910. (From the Hogg
Collection; reproduced by permission of the Ulster Museum).

Robert Sawyers (right) with his wife and some of their family
with other children in front of his grocery and hardware
business at Christmas *c.* 1928. Mrs Sawyers recently celebrated
her 91st birthday. She came to Aughnacloy in 1919 on her
marriage to Robert Sawyers.

Michael Daly came to Aughnacloy *c.* 1902. His emporium had a millinery department on the first floor, where 3 or 4 girls were constantly employed. Mr Daly later became a J.P. for County Tyrone.

Clogher *c.* 1930 showing the Commons with Bailey's blacksmith's forge in the centre. Ned Moan's forge is seen at the bottom of the Pound Brae (near the cart). The Cathedral, built in 1744, dominates the scene, as in most photographs of Clogher. (From the Green Collection; reproduced by permission of the Ulster Folk & Transport Museum).

Main Street, Clogher *c.* 1910. Johnston Bros shop (by the lamp) was instrumental in bringing many of the latest implements and farm machinery into general use in the Valley. A Pierce No 8 Mowing Machine stands by the kerb.

Augher Creamery *c.* 1910. The Creamery was opened in 1898
and was supplied by farmers using a milk train as well as the
self carters shown here. A goods wagon standing at the goods
shed can be seen in the right background.

32

Fivemiletown also had its Co-op named after Ballylurgan the former name of the town.

Main Street, Fivemiletown *c. 1923*. The CVR makes its way
through the town while a steam roller (in foreground) is
engaged in surfacing the street.

David Graham's shop, Fivemiletown *c.* 1895. Graham along
with H de F Montgomery was the principal promoter of the
railway at Fivemiletown.

Ballygawley c. 1880. This view of the Main Street taken from Ballygawley bridge shows the brewery on the left and the distillery on the right. Most of the town's population seem to be quite overawed by the appearance of a camera on this particular day.

Fair Day in Ballygawley *c.* 1936.
This view looks down Meeting
Street towards the Omagh Road.

RURAL LIFE

BY THE CLOSE of the nineteenth century most of the farm work was still done by hand. Spade labour was common up until the years of the First World War and the iron swing plough was confined to the better soil of the Valley floor. Here the 'swing' itself was gradually being ousted by the 'chill'—a chilled steel plough with a wheel riding on the score. Ploughing was the hallmark of a good farm and there was always great interest in the competition afforded by the annual ploughing matches. *The Tyrone Constitution* reported over 600 onlookers at the 1871 ploughing match held at Aughentaine Castle. These events, generally organised by the Clogher Farming Society or its successors, remained an important social event in the community until the mid 1930s when the arrival of the tractors killed the interest.

There was little haymaking machinery before 1900 with most of the work done with the scythe. On the bigger farms or on a landlord's estate an Albion, Pierce or a Ransome mowing machine might be seen. Oats were cut with the scythe or the hook for the best part of the nineteenth century, and it was not until the 1880s that a reaper pulled by a four horse team had made its appearance. These heavy implements were not known beyond the fields of the gentry until after the Great War, when modifications to them had reduced their weight to two-horse binders, making them available to many of the substantial infield farms. Threshing was done with the flail on most farms before 1900. By then, however, the horse-powered barn thresher was becoming popular even on moderately sized farms. These threshers were turned by a pony ring and gearing fitted up outside. The gearing on William Bryan's farm at Lungs had a double arm to accommodate two horses or even four if necessary.

The scots cart was the universal transport used, and even on the smaller farms they often had one made to suit a donkey if they did not possess a horse. The spring cart or the roundabout trap was used on more formal occasions, providing transport to church, to the fairs or for Sunday visiting. Wealthier families had the use of gigs or dogcarts and the local gentry might have risen to a phaeton or a Brougham. The first tractors appeared at the end of the First World War. Colebrooke Estate and Thomas S. Porter at Clogher Park each had a Fordson by 1919, and P. R. Peebles of Killycorran had an International a year or two later. It was not until 1937 that the Ferguson-Brown appeared. Henry Johnston of Annagarvey and Major Moutray of Favour Royal had the first two in the Valley. The firm of Johnston Bros of Clogher were early agents for Harry Ferguson and were instrumental in importing most of the area's first tractors as well as a good range of hay making implements. (See photograph on page 31).

The saving of the hay crop was an essential operation each summer, and there was a considerable amount of 'swopping' of labour to do it. Few made silage though there was some interest in it in the last two decades of the nineteenth century. The local pioneers were T. S. Porter at Clogher Park, Dr J. B. Story of Corick and the Rev T. G. Stokes of Aughnacloy. It was an operation that required a large amount of labour and few ordinary farmers had the resources to try it. By 1900 it had almost been abandoned and Mr Stokes was the only farmer not just in the Valley but in Tyrone who made it. Silage making made brief reappearances during the First World War (at Clogher Park and at Aughentaine Castle) but did not become a permanent aspect of farming until the early 1950s when a series of wet summers made it practical.

On many of the smaller holdings oats were cut with the smooth
hook. Here Ellen and Mary McCaughney are seen working
barefoot at Corleaghan. (Rose Shaw collection, by courtesy of
Ulster Folk & Transport Museum).

Haymaking *c.* 1910. The Bogues in Ballymacan and their neighbours take a rest from the arduous task of hand raking. Brackenridge's monument is on the skyline to their South West. (Rose Shaw collection).

Haymaking again, but 20 years later and on a lowland farm.
This picture taken near Augher shows one horse with a
tumbling paddy and the other behind pulling a horse-drawn
hay rake. Horse drawn implements speeded up the saving of
the hay crop and took the drudgery out of the work.

A typical thatched farmhouse above Fardross. Most of the smaller farmhouses were single-storied three roomed dwellings, with sometimes a low loft for additional sleeping quarters (note small gable window here) or a bed-outshot from the back wall of the kitchen. (Rose Shaw collection).

Carntall House *c.* 1910. This long slated farmhouse represented
the sort of home a substantial gentleman-farmer occupied.
George Mills, who farmed 90 acres is seen here with his wife by
the front door. This house, which no longer exists, was burnt in
1932.

Joseph Mayne holding a plough at the 1934 ploughing match at Springfield. At 75 years of age he was the oldest ploughman on the field. Ploughing matches were very popular and on this occasion there were 25 entries.

Ploughing matches lapsed in 1912 and were not revived again until 1931. Here the organizing committee pose for the camera at the front of Brookvale where the 1931 match was held. The group includes (front row) Col. A. U. Gledstanes, Sir Basil Brooke M.P. (third from left) Thomas Richey (centre) and William Watson (extreme right).

Patrick McCaughey and his wife Catherine making ridges in Ballymacan 1906. Potatoes were set in lazy beds on many of the smaller mountain farms. (Rose Shaw collection).

John Johnston, the author's father, seen driving the first Ferguson-Brown tractor in use in the Valley. This tractor, which was the fourth of its kind issued in County Tyrone was purchased by the Johnstons in 1937. It was the first small tractor to be fitted with the hydraulic system and within a few years had revolutionised farming all over Ulster.

Bristol Caterpillar moulding potatoes at Corboe, 1937. The tractor, purchased in 1936 was owned jointly by James Thompson (seen driving here) and his brother-in-law, Robert Smith of Tullyvernon.

Stewards and committee of Clogher Valley Show *c.* 1928.
Andrew J. Richardson of Farnetra, who was the Secretary, is
third from the left standing, while at the front (on right) are
Capt. J. H. King (with whip) and Thomas McLaren,
auctioneer.

The crowd waiting for the next event at the 1908 Show at
Clogher Park.

PEOPLE AND EVENTS

THE MAIN EVENTS in the calendar in the early years of this century were the Clogher Valley Show and the Twelfth of July. Hibernians paraded on Lady Day (15th August) and the Blackmen on the Twelfth of August. After 1919 an annual Remembrance Day parade and service organised through the British Legion added another event to the calendar. Days out were confined beyond this to Bank Holiday excursions or to the festivities connected with a royal visit to the province. Concerts, dances and soirées were very much of a fund-raising rather than a social nature, though in some cases reached grander dimensions. Fivemiletown had a string orchestra in the early 1920s while Aughnacloy had its music hall in the 1880s.

Elections created considerable interest from time to time especially when there was a split in the vote. In 1885 South Tyrone became a separate constituency and elected William O'Brien a prominent Nationalist as its M.P. This was something of a surprise and the following year the seat was captured by T. W. Russell, standing as a Liberal Unionist. Russell, however, alienated the landlord interest and found himself opposed by a Unionist, Andrew Horner KC, in 1906. There was a lot of tension as Russell switched parties, taking with him a core of about 300 Presbyterian farmers (the Russellites) who enabled him to hold on to his seat with Nationalist support. However, four years later Horner recaptured the seat amid scenes of great excitement. Sixty extra police were called to Clogher Courthouse to deal with the count and that evening there was stone throwing at Aughnacloy while the Valley was set alight with loyalist bonfires.

After Horner's death in 1916 William Coote held the seat without incident. In the Northern Ireland parliament the Unionists held Tyrone South comfortably and at times without being opposed at all. The only real challenge to Rowley Elliott in these years was in 1929 when J. J. Haslett of Cottagehill, an Independent Unionist, polled 4,600 votes. The loyalists burned an effigy of Haslett at Crilly. The Unionists retained the same control in local government except for a brief period between 1906 and 1910 when the Russellites gained control of Clogher Union.

Clogher Board of Guardians in front of the Workhouse *c*. 1906.
Standing (left to right) Thomas Turner (Clerk of the Union)
George McElroy Jun. (Solicitor), William Kirkpatrick,
Owen Lynch, George McElroy J.P., M. J. Fiddes J.P., Samuel
Richey, John Connolly and W. C. Trimble *(Impartial Reporter)*.
Seated, H. T. Armstrong, George McAlpine, Patrick
Campbell, James McLaren J.P., Hugh de F. Montgomery
D.L., J.P., William Richey, W. J. Jones J.P., Joseph Smith,
David Wright and Patrick McGirr.

Cardinal MacRory conferring confirmation in BallyMacElroy
Church *c.* 1939. His Eminence Joseph Cardinal MacRory was
a native of the Ballygawley district and was born at Shantavney
in 1861. He was Bishop of Down and Connor from 1915 and
Primate of All Ireland from 1928. He died in 1945.

Fardross Band *c.* 1900. Most of the bands associated with the
Orange Order were flute bands (generally called 'Part' bands)
in the early days. It was only in the last fifty years that pipe and
silver bands made real headway against them. The flute band
was popular because the instruments were inexpensive and the
'uniforms' easy to come by.

Teamakers at Clogher Courthouse on Remembrance Sunday 1929. Back row (left to right): Mrs McCaffrey, Mrs Keane, Mrs Buchanan, Mrs Stanford (with child), Canon Keane, Mrs Williamson and Miss Carrie Murphy. Front row: Mrs G. Downey and son, Miss Steen, Mrs Johnston, Mrs Stockdale (with medals), Stewart Buchanan, Mrs Steen, Mrs Morrow and Iris Morrow.

Carntall National School 1914. Back row (left to right):—
Smith, Joseph Cullinan, —McClean, Arnold Holden,
Marshall Holden, J. Graham, Jim Beatty and Master G. B.
Sloan. Middle row: Miss Sweeney, Teresa McConnell, Olive
Stockdale, Minnie Adams, Jane Cullinan, Dorothy Stockdale,
Sally McConnell, Maggie Barr and Tom Stockdale. Front
row:—Smiton, Hannah Adams, —McCombe, A Clifford,
Sally Holden, Annie Holland, Millie Stockdale, Martha Adams
and John Beatty. Carntall new school, which was built at
Carntall Cross in 1891, was under Presbyterian management.

Ballyscally National School *c.* 1922. It was under the management of the Parish Priest of Clogher.
Back Row: Bridget McCaffrey, Mary McCaffrey, Maud Metthewson, Annie McElroy, Lena McCarroll, Letty McCarroll, Mary McCluskey, Gerry McCaffrey, Peter McCaffrey, Albert Corrigan and Tom Nolan.
2nd Row: Miss Smith (later Mrs McGarrity), Sarah McCaughey, Annie McCarroll, Mary McKenna, Susan McKenna, Eileen McCluskey, Bernadette McCafrey, Ellen McElroy, Owen McKenna, Mickey Corrigan, John Corrigan, John Keys and Packie Devine with Master Francis Doogan (Principal)

3rd Row: Pat McConnell, Mary Donaghy, Theresa McElroy, Annie McCaughey, Eva Keys, Rose McElroy, Bridget McCaffrey, Bridget Corrigan, Molly McKenna, Mary McCaughey, Rose Corrigan, Kitty McKenna and Mary McKenna.
Front Row: Pat Lowry, Pat McCaffrey, Jimmy McCaffrey, Packie McElroy, Peter F McConnell, Jim McCluskey, Clarence Corrigan, Eamon McKenna, John McCaughey, Pat McKenna, Frankie Shields, John F McConnell and Jimmy McCarroll.

56

Sir James Craig with Lord Derby (second from right in front)
at the time of the Border Commission's visit to Fivemiletown
in 1925. Dr Samuel Bleakley and Hugh de F Montgomery D.L.
are in front on Lord Derby's left. Jacob Tavener and Mr R. S.
Anderson are on Sir James Craig's right.

Clogher Valley B Specials at Fardross House *c.* 1930.

Fivemiletown String Orchestra *c.* 1918. Left to right: Maggie
Gillespie, Carrie Brannigan, Catherine Anderson, Mrs
Gillespie (hotelier), W. J. Gillespie, Jim Martin, Miss Elliott
and Pat Tierney (watchmaker and photographer).

INDUSTRY

BY THE TIME the Railway opened in 1887 the days of domestic spinning and weaving were almost over. Flax provided a lot of employment in the early and mid nineteenth century and as late as 1871, 17 scutching mills were still in operation. The womenfolk on many of the smaller farms derived a valuable ancillary income from spinning the flax yarn either for their own use or in supplying merchants from outside the Valley. Home weaving among these farmers and among the labouring class had also been a good source of income during the long winter evenings. The great factories of Britain could now produce cotton garments as cheaply as any made locally with the result that by 1890 there was scarcely a weaver here at work on his loom.

In 1864 George Vesey Stewart set up a large three-storied spinning mill at Lisdoart. He employed over 200 there and went on to develop the site with a ropewalk and 30-stock tow scutching mill as well as a terrace of brick-built houses for his workers. Stewart ran his own market for fresh vegetables and dairy produce on the site and opened a factory shop where the currency used was his own ''quoits'' which came in denominations of a penny, a shilling and a half crown. He overstretched himself, however, and his mill closed in the 1880s. It was not reopened until 1900 when a Cavan businessman, William Coote—later M.P. for the area—founded the Lisdoart Woollen Mills making tweeds, rugs and blankets. Coote also started a woollen factory at Clogher in 1918 in premises that were once part of the old workhouse, and began a hosiery factory at Aughnacloy about the same time. Coote's mill at Clogher became a shirt factory in the early 1930s using the trade name 'Somax'.

Mrs H. de F. Montgomery was a great patron of craft work in Fivemiletown towards the end of the nineteenth century. In 1875 she started a class for plain sewing and embroidery for women. Encouraged by her success she embarked on a scheme of repoussé metal work for men and boys in 1892. She taught the class herself and in 1901 opened a shop and workshop in the Main Street. Previously the men had worked in their spare time but now some of them took it up full-time. They worked mainly in copper and brass and by 1908 had taken up silver work and enamelling as well. The industry, which was known locally as the 'Copper Shop', flourished until the early years of the War when a lot of the men enlisted.

Ballygawley had been a thriving industrial site in the mid nineteenth century when the brewery and distillery were in full swing. Both were run by the Armstrong family under the patronage of the Stewarts of Ballygawley Park. The distillery, which stood on the premises now occupied by Loughran's garage once covered an area of forty five thousand square feet, while the brewery—more or less across the Street from it—had a malt house that was almost a hundred feet long. By 1880 both were gone.

Mary Maguire, Kell, probably the last operative spinner in the
Valley.

The Art Metal class at Fivemiletown, photographed outside Sam Carruth's house. Mr Carruth is standing by the door and on his left stands Paddy Roche who earned a high reputation as a silversmith at various R.D.S. exhibitions. Roche made a pair of silver rose bowls for Primate Crozier about 1908.

Lisdoart Spinning Mill after it had become a woollen factory.

Ballygawley's brewery (on the left) and distillery (behind street on right) *c.* 1878. The distillery was sold in 1873 and the brewery ceased operations a few years afterwards. (This photograph and the one on the opposite page may well be the work of Lawrence).

The staff and employees of the brewery *c.* 1878.

SPORT AND LEISURE

THERE WAS LITTLE organised sport in the Valley before 1880. In fact it was not considered manly or worthwhile to take time off from one's work to indulge in either exercise or pleasure. However things gradually changed and a keen following of football and handball developed by the turn of the century, with the Hunt providing the principal recreation for the landowners and gentlemen farmers. Children played marbles and skittles and there was considerable interest in Irish dancing. Like their elders they also played handball and soccer. Aughnacloy had a ball alley as early as 1860 and in the other towns a tall gable filled the need.

Football was the most popular sport, however, and from 1902 was competitively organised. Augher Stars, Clogher Hibernians and Fivemiletown played for the Clogher Valley Cup in these pre First World War days, while in later years it was the Mercer Cup or the Coffey Cup that they competed for. Often these sides had junior teams and there were teams in country places like Crieve and Cavanaleck as well. Cricket made its first appearance about 1868 and there were teams at Clogher, Aughnacloy and Fivemiletown at various stages over the next 70 years. A golf club was formed at Aughnacloy with links at Annagh in 1888 and another at Clogher in 1904. Fivemiletown also got a links about 1923. Within a few years it had a thriving hockey club. Gaelic football was first organized at Aughnacloy in 1904 and before long had clubs at Ballygawley and Augher. An Augher player, Ned McGee, brought honour and distinction to the game in the Valley when he was capped for Tyrone and eventually for Ulster. The Tyrone Hunt had the patronage of most of the local gentry and hunted right across the Valley. It was allowed to peter out during the First World War but was replaced by the Seskanore Harriers which regularly hunted over Aughentaine, Cecil and Fardross.

No one took holidays except the gentry before the days of the railway. In fact the Bank Holiday excursions on the tram linking up with the broad gauge systems at Tynan or Maguiresbridge provided the first glimpse of the sea not just for the Valley's children, but for many of its adults as well. These outings to Bundoran or Warrenpoint were the only holiday most families had until motor cars made the family holiday a more realistic prospect in the inter-war years. Church sports and picnics, sometimes accompanied by a trip on the tram to an ancient castle or some landlord's demesne were also popular. There is an interesting photograph of Ballygawley Band of Hope with Lisbeg Band setting out for a picnic in a nearby field in 1927. Roman Catholic children had sports on some holy days and in Clogher parish there was always a large gathering at the annual sports at Altadavin Wood on Bilberry Sunday. The Boy Scouts came to Fivemiletown before the First World War and in later years there were troops at Clogher and Aughnacloy as well. Cycling was also popular and one of the features of the Clogher Valley Show's annual gymkhana was its bicycle races, for both youths and adults. Greyhound racing had some following in the Augher district and there were events for ponies and horses on a regular basis all over the Valley. The C.V.R. generally ran an excursion train to these meetings on Easter Mondays.

A • Social • Entertainment

IN CONNECTION WITH THE
Augher Branch of the Total Abstinence Union
WILL BE HELD IN THE
PROTESTANT HALL, AUGHER,
On Thursday Evening, the 10th of March, 1910.

TEA AT 7.30 O'CLOCK, P.M.

An Interesting Programme will be gone through.

ADMISSION, GENTLEMEN,   SIXPENCE.

AUGHER
CYCLING CLUB.

SEASON 1909.

PROMOTION OF

SPORT, ROAD-RIDING,

TOURING, RACING,
AND
GOODFELLOWSHIP.

5349—Impartial Reporter

FIVEMILETOWN
GOLF CLUB.

FIVEMILETOWN, Co. TYRONE.

COMPETITIONS FOR 1925

9003—F. Times, Enniskillen

Fivemiletown Comrades
Football Club.

Member's Ticket,
1920-21.

Captain,   N. Hetherington,
Vice-Captain,   R. Ancketell,
Sec. and Treas.   R. S. Tevener.

1901. Fermanag Time

67

KNOCKMANY CARN, AUGHER, TYRONE.   R.W. 1916.

Knockmany Chambered Cairn 1898 (From the Welch Collection, Ulster Museum). Picnics on the top of Knockmany were popular for family outings on Sundays or Bank Holidays. The young girl here is Miss Dorothy Gervais of Cecil Manor, then aged 13. Knockmany Hill which became one of the first state forests in Northern Ireland, was landscaped and first planted by her great-grandfather, the Rev. Francis Gervais who purchased the Cecil estate in 1811.

Other favourite picnic sites were Brackenridge's Monument (above), and St Patrick's Chair (right). The tower was built in 1847 by George Brackenridge, a small landowner and local magistrate who in 1839 had taken the name of his maternal grandmother for that of Trimble. St Patrick's Chair is in Altadavin Glen close to Favour Royal estate. It is reputed to have been a Druidic site before St Patrick made it a Christian altar. There is a large altar stone here and a holy well below it. Miss Gladys Moutray of Summerhill is the figure seated in the chair. The top photograph was taken in 1923 and the chair in 1907.

Ballygawley Presbyterian Church Band of Hope headed by Lisbeg Band *en route* for their annual picnic *c.* 1922. The minister of Ballygawley congregation, Rev. Richard Park, is in conversation with Mr William Burton, a church elder. The Band of Hope was founded in Leeds shortly after 1850 by Mary Jane Carlisle and aimed at promoting ideas of temperance among the young.

Fivemiletown Boy Scouts at Downhill *c.* 1924. The group
includes the troop's founder Major-General Hugh Maude de F.
Montgomery (in front of the door on right) and beside him the
scoutmaster, Mr Samuel Breadon.

Fivemiletown Football Club with the Mulhern Cup 1933. Back row (left to right): W. Sloan, W. Johnston, P. McCaffrey, T. N. Morrison, Tom Montgomery, R. S. Tavener. Middle row: D. McCaffrey, J.P., W. Porter, H Torrens, —Montgomery, —Taylor, E. Fenton and W. Shields. Front row: Jim Boyd, —Montgomery, —Boyd, Major-General H. M. de F. Montgomery, Reggie Boyd and Robin O'Malley.

72

Ned McGee of Clogher, who was capped several times for Ulster at Gaelic football, pictured here with the Railway Cup for inter-provincial competition, *c.* 1942.

There were golf clubs at Aughnacloy, Clogher and
Fivemiletown. Aughnacloy opened in 1888, Clogher in 1904
and this one, seen here at Fivemiletown, about 1923.

Aughentaine Parish camogie team 1935. Camogie was first played locally at Ballygawley in 1933. A team was formed in Aughnacloy (Moybridge) in 1934 and a third at Aughentaine in the same year. This side which played in Cullinan's field at Gortmore includes (Back row, left—right) Ellen McCarney, Mary Gunn, Winnie McGearey and Brigid Owens. In front are Bridie Droogan, Peggy Gunn, Etta Finlay, Brigid McCarney, Agnes Droogan and an unknown player.

CLOGHER VALLEY TRAMWAY.

TYNAN
HUNT
RACES.

ON EASTER MONDAY,

30th MARCH, 1891,

EXCURSION TICKETS

will be issued by the following SPECIAL and ORDINARY
Trains to CALEDON, viz. :

STATIONS.		A.M.	A.M.	RETURN FARES.	
				1st Cl	3rd Cl.
MAGUIRESBRIDGE	dep.		9.54		
BROOKEBORO'	,,		10.8	3/6	2/3
FIVEMILETOWN	,,		10.42	3/0	2/0
CLOGHER	,,	8.57	11.22	2/6	1/8
AUGHER	,,	9.5	11.31		
BALLYGAWLEY	,,	9.25	11.58	2/3	1/6
AUGHNACLOY	,,	9.55	12.24	1/8	1/2

Tickets are not Transferable and are available for Return only on day
of issue by the following Trains. viz :—ORDINARY TRAIN leaving
Tynan at 6.30 p.m., RUNNING THROUGH to MAGUIRESBRIDGE,
if required ; and SPECIAL TRAIN leaving Tynan at 8.10 p.m., arriving at Aughnacloy at 8.50 p.m., Ballygawley 9.10 p.m., Augher 9.30 p.m.,
Clogher 9.38 p.m., and Fivemiletown 10.13 p.m.

NO LUGGAGE ALLOWED.

By Order,

D. J. STEWART,
General Manager.

Head Office, Aughnacloy,
28th Feb., 1891.

4077   Printed at the Enniskillen Gas-Power Printing Works.

Clogher Valley Agricultural Society's Show,

THURSDAY, 18TH AUGUST, 1910.

PROGRAMME

— OF —

HORSE-JUMPING, RIDING, DRIVING, &c.,
COMPETITIONS,

— IN —

CLOGHER PARK,

Commencing at Three o'clock, p.m.

PRESIDENT :
THOMAS S. PORTER, Esq.

JUDGES :
Horse Events
THE RIGHT HON. F. WRENCH, DUBLIN.
COLONEL J. K. M'CLINTOCK, SESKINORE, OMAGH.

Dancing
MR. PHILIP WALDRON, KILSKEERY, TRILLICK.

Starters—Dr. Warnock, Mr. Turner.
Lap Keepers—Mr. John Reid, Mr. C. Evans.
Stewards—Dr. Warnock, Messrs. Thomas Turner, W. Stewart, J. Morrow,
Willie Richey, A. M. Steen, E. R. Rice, Henry Johnston, R.
Cuthbertson, D. Irwin, P. Hughes, John Bryan, J. Cull
J. Little, J. Short, C. Evans, F. M'Carroll,
and John Reid,
Committee—Dr. Warnock, Messrs. Thomas Turner, William Stewart, John
Johnston, John Bryan, A. J. Richardson, P. Johnston,
R. Cuthbertson, and Henry Johnston.
Treasurer—Thomas Turner.
Secretary—A. J. Richardson.

PROGRAMME, - - TWOPENCE.

The South Tyrone Hunt at Aughentaine Castle *c.* 1913.
Unfortunately it has not been possible to name many, but the
group includes several of those listed as Stewards and
Committee Members on the 1910 Show Programme (opposite
page). The compiler's grandfather, Henry Johnston is the
stoutish man in the very centre.

THE BIG HOUSE

THE CLOGHER VALLEY, although it had no really large landowner, had its fair share of big houses and estates. These houses provided a great deal of employment locally, from the landsteward down to kitchen maids or footmen. At one point in time the Moutrays of Favour Royal—who were the Valley's largest landowners—were giving employment to eighty people. This whole array of people included butlers, gardeners, tutors, gamekeepers and chauffeurs as well as kitchen maids, parlour maids and dairy maids. The stewards themselves were an interesting section of the community, as they came from so many different areas and from so many different backgrounds. Many of them remained in the area and became large farmers, often employing a range of servants themselves. Indeed in one instance a steward (John Smith) was eventually evicted or driven out by his former employer (T. R. Browne of Aughentaine Castle) because of the intense jealousy his prosperity had engendered between them.

Relations between landlord and tenant were good, mainly because most of the proprietors were resident farmers themselves. The Orange Order helped to identify the landlords socially with the rank and file of the majority of their Protestant tenants. Even the Land League was not able to drive a wedge between them though there was some discontent in the 1880s. John Wardlow Johnston of Ivy Hill was the only landlord in the area to have a serious attempt made on his life. Children were frequently named after their landlord as a mark of respect and generally speaking the local gentry had the welfare of their tenants at heart.

The big houses of the Clogher Valley were invariably interlinked through marriage and this provided for considerable social intercouse outside the normal parochial and sporting meetings. John Corry Moutray of Favour Royal had daughters married and living in Augher Castle and Killyfaddy while his sister, Isabella, was the wife of Whitney Gledstanes and the mistress of Fardross House. One of his sons was married to a Miss Stewart of Martray Manor and there were close ties of blood through several generations between his family and the Anketells of Anketell Grove, not far from Aughnacloy but in County Monaghan. On the other hand families like the Montgomerys of Blessingbourne and the Storys of Corick looked beyond the Valley for their careers and social life while still retaining a powerful interest in it. Two of the Montgomerys became famous soldiers and Dr J. B. Story became a distinguished Dublin oculist at the turn of the century.

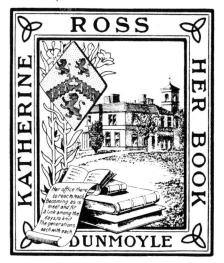

ROSS
KATHERINE
HER BOOK
DUNMOYLE

Her office there
to reach to teach
Becoming as is
meet and fit
A link among the
days to knit
The generations
each with each

Bookplate of Katherine, Lady Ross, Dunmoyle Castle, near Ballygawley.

Croquet on the Deanery Lawn, Clogher, 1908. The families trying their skill here are the Moutrays of Summerhill and the Haire-Fosters. The Very Rev. Arthur Newburgh Haire-Foster, who was Dean from 1911, occupied the Deanery as Rector of Clogher from 1900 until 1925.

Favour Royal. This was the new house built by John Corry
Moutray in 1825 to replace the old 1670 house destroyed by fire
in 1823. The Moutrays were the largest landowners in the
Valley and at one time held a rental of 36 townlands.

Shooting syndicate at Favour Royal 1932. Three of the Valley's principal landowners are seen in front: Major Anketell Gerald Moutray, Col. Ambrose U. Gledstanes (of Fardross) and Capt. Harvey Knox-Browne of Aughentaine Castle. The young girl at left is Miss Rosemary (Roguie) Moutray who became an Irish Lawn Tennis champion.

Augher Castle, May 1905. (From the Hogg Collection,
reproduced by permission the Ulster Museum)

On the front steps at Killybrick *c.* 1907. Killybrick was the
second of three substantial houses built by the Moutrays within
Favour Royal desmesne. At this time it was occupied by
unmarried sisters of the owner of Favour Royal.

Moutray shooting party with beaters at lunch on Bragan hill
*c.*1907.

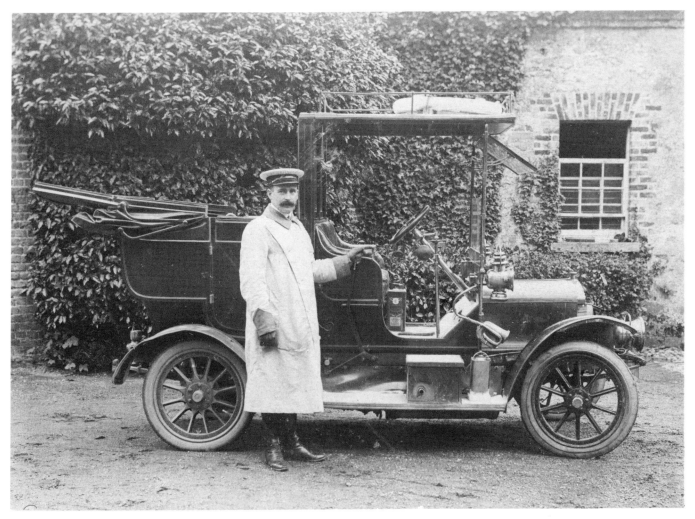

Henry Charters and car, June 1912. Charters was chauffeur to
Sir John Ross at Dunmoyle Castle. Sir John was a
distinguished lawyer and the last Lord Chancellor of Ireland
1921-22.

ACKNOWLEDGEMENTS

IN COMPILING a work of this nature I have to thank a large number of people, who either took or possess the photographs used. Their readiness to part with their treasures for a considerable period has been greatly appreciated. In acknowledging those whose photographs are shown here I am mindful of the many others whose material might almost as easily have been chosen.

The two private collections that I used most are those of Dr George Gillespie and the late Mr Alec Bennoch. Dr Gillespie has had a keen eye and ear for everything in the Valley for close on sixty years now, and any work about it both now and in the future will be heavily indebted to him. Mr Alec Bennoch gathered a fascinating display of photographs and memorabilia in his shop in Fivemiletown, and I am grateful to his son, Brian, for the use of several of them.

The photographs of the railway, apart from those held by Armagh County Museum and Dr Gillespie, come mainly from the collections of two railway enthusiasts, Dr Ted Patterson and Mr Tom McDevitte. I also wish to thank the following for the use of material in their possession, or for procuring photographs for this selection: Mr Jim Adams and his sister Miss Jean Adams, Augher Creamery, Miss Helga Bailey, Mrs Amy Barnett, Miss Monica Brady, Mrs Evelyn Boyd, Mr B. M.Hackett M.P.S., Mr Alec Hunter, Mr John Holmes (Monasterevan), Mr Gerry Loughran, Mr P. K. Lynch, Mrs E. R. Martin, Mr James Mills, Miss June Mehaul, Miss Brigid McCarney, Mr Mick McElroy, Miss Ruby McKeown, Mr Tom McKeagney, Mrs Margaret McConnell, Mr Walter Noble, Dean Nevil O'Neill, Mr Baden Priestly, Mr Adrian Robinson, Mr Bob Sawyers, Miss Millie Stockdale, Mr George Sloan and Mr Thomas Trimble. I am indebted to Dr Edward McParland for identifying the building in the photograph of the scouts (page 71).

Finally I am grateful to the following public bodies for the use of photographs: Armagh County Museum (and in particular to its Curator, Mr D. R. M. Weatherup), the Public Record Office of Northern Ireland, the trustees of the Ulster Museum (the Welch and Hogg collections), the trustees of the Ulster Folk and Transport Museum (the Green and Rose Shaw collections) and to Dungannon District Council whose photographer Mr Mark Mohan made copies of some material on limited loan. He also drew the map on page v. The District Council were helpful in that they gave my publishers a generous grant towards the publication costs. But for their assistance the book would not be available at such a competitive price and in such an attractive format.

Ratory, Clogher
June 1987.

FURTHER READING

SOURCES on the Clogher Valley covering this period are difficult to obtain nowadays. John J. Marshall's two little histories *Clochar Na Righ* (Dungannon, 1930) and the *Annals of Aughnacloy* (2nd edn, Dungannon, 1925) are over 50 years out of print. Rose Shaw's *Carleton's country* (Dublin, 1930) is likewise a scarce item as is the two volume history of the Catholic diocese of Clogher, *Parishes of Clogher* (Enniskillen, 1920) by Canon James E. MacKenna. A contemporary historian Canon J. B.Leslie covered the same ground for the Church of Ireland parishes in his *Clogher clergy and parishes* (Enniskillen, 1929). All of these sources were written within a single decade. Nothing significant appeared for a further 27 years until Benedict Kiely produced his *Poor Scholar* (Dublin, 1947) which was a study of the life and work of William Carleton. The most recent historical study of the area is of course Dr E. M. Patterson's much acclaimed book *The Clogher Valley Railway* which deals largely with the railway but which also gives pleasant little sketches of each of the towns and villages. In the same year (1972) Dr Rosemary Harris produced her fascinating study of Ballygawley and district, *Prejudice and tolerance in Ulster*.

Recent sources come mainly from articles in *Clogher Record*, the journal of Clogher Historical Society, from a few numbers of *Seanchas Ardmhaca* (the journal of Armagh Historical Society) and from two articles in *Ulster Folklife*. Here the contributors include Dr George Gillespie, Rev Brendan MacEvoy, Dr D. B. McNeill and myself. In addition to material in the learned journals there are a good range of recent church histories.